UNDERNEATH THE LINTEL

An Impressive Presentation of Lovely Evidences

Glen Berger

BROADWAY PLAY PUBLISHING INC
224 E 62nd St, NY, NY 10065
www.broadwayplaypub.com
info@broadwayplaypub.com

UNDERNEATH THE LINTEL
© Copyright 2003 by Glen Berger

First printing: May 2003, Second printing
   (revised): July 2006, This printing: Sept 2011
trade edition I S B N: 978-0-88145-223-5
Book design: Marie Donovan
Word processing: Microsoft Word for Windows
Typographic controls: Ventura Publisher 2.0 P E
Typeface: Palatino
Printed and bound in the U S A

UNDERNEATH THE LINTEL premiered Off-Broadway at the Soho Playhouse, opening on October 23, 2001, and produced by Scott Morfee, Tom Wirtshafter, and Dana Matthow. The cast and creative contributors were:

THE LIBRARIAN .... T Ryder Smith

Director .... Randy White
Set design .... Lauren Helpern
Projection design consultant ..... Elaine McCarthy
Lighting design .... Tyler Micoleau
Sound design .... Paul Adams
Costume .... Miranda Hoffman
Production stage manager .... Richard Hodge
Production coordinator .... Cris Buchner

In January 2002, David Chandler took over the role of THE LIBRARIAN.

UNDERNEATH THE LINTEL was first presented
at the Yale Summer Cabaret, in New Haven,
for three nights in August 1999, with the author
playing THE LIBRARIAN.

UNDERNEATH THE LINTEL was produced
by The Actors' Gang, Patti McGuire, producer,
in Los Angeles for a limited run in May 2001.
The cast and creative contributors were:

THE LIBRARIAN .... Brian T Finney

Director & designer .... Brent Hinkley

Stage manager .... Byrne Lethnik

SETTING & CHARACTER

Setting: Here

Time: Now

Set: THE LIBRARIAN has rented the space for
the night, and didn't have much to spend on it.
Perhaps the auditorium we're in has been "dark"
for some time, or perhaps the theater is "between
shows". Props and other detritus from other
shows can litter the back of the stage, or be seen in
an exposed back room. An air of dilapidation
would be fine. Perhaps THE LIBRARIAN is giving
this lecture in a seedier part of town, on a rainy
night, to four or five down-and-outs more
interested in getting dry from the rain than
listening to a lecture by a Dutchman. Over the
course of the evening however, the "lecture"
should imperceptibly turn into "theater". The
detritus, unnoticed and seemingly unimportant
at first, can unexpectedly take on significance,
alluding to scenes and history mentioned in the
play. The lighting can become warmer, more
"theatrical", etc, and what seemed like a random
strewing of objects, or a random water stain on the
wall, for instance, can turn out to be not so random
after all.

Character: Dutch because: The Dutch have a wonderfully bureaucratic streak in them (or so I'm told). They also tend to have a facility for other European languages, and I've known more than one person from the Netherlands who had remarkable English, with a nearly imperceptible accent. Point is, the accent should be very light, and the actor should pay more attention to developing the "idiolect", meaning "an individual's unique way of speaking".

Like the set, the character should imperceptibly transform over the evening.

One last note: THE LIBRARIAN's narrative is written, generally, in the past tense. However, the less the narrative is actually presented in the past tense, the better. Immediacy, I think, is key to giving this play some theatrical life. As THE LIBRARIAN narrates how he found a claim ticket in the Baedeker's, for instance, he can "find" the claim ticket all over again.

Without sacrificing pacing, of course, the goal is to make THE LIBRARIAN's saga, in the end, nothing like a lecture, but rather, something that is happening now.

(Stage contains a chair [which should never be used for sitting], a large chalkboard [to be used at director's discretion]. There is also a battered screen for showing slides, the slide projector to be operated by the actor. A rather old and disheveled man in decrepit suit shuffles onto the stage carrying a battered suitcase full of scraps. The suitcase, once open, may have various homemade contrivances to display the "evidences."

([Perhaps, over the course of the play, he also keeps certain evidences in his pockets, with evidence tags dangling out.] He wears a date stamper tied with string around his neck.)

LIBRARIAN: So. Right. We'll proceed. I have only one night for this. I would like to have more, oh yes, but due to the extortionary rates demanded by the proprietors of this auditorium...I have only one night for this. Still. We'll proceed. *(He points significantly to suitcase he has set down.)* Box of scraps. *Significant* scraps. Or rather...they're all I have...to *prove* a life.... To prove one life...and justify another...and if you're thinking "that's a tall order for a box of scraps," well just you wait. *(With ominous significance)* They're not just scraps. *(Announcing) An Impressive Presentation of Lovely Evidences.* Hold on to your hats, gentlemen. Bonnets, ladies. *(Suddenly realizing) Hold on...* *(Scanning seats) ...is this all there is? (Despair and*

indignation) I don't know what more I can do!
I put up signs, I did, on the poles, "Impressive
Presentation!" but as soon as I turn my back,
they're plastered over! With other signs! And
mine were nicer. And important. And tomorrow,
I'll be gone.... *(Pondering it on a more personal level—)*
...in no time at all...I'll be gone.... *(But pulls himself
out of it)* ...Still. We'll proceed.

I am...a librarian. From Hoofddorp, that's Holland.
Or rather, I was, before I was fired. Or rather,
I retired. Against my will. Without my pension.
Or rather, that's none of your business. Or rather,
it will be, but not yet. My special duty for more
than many years being to check in the books
that came in overnight through the overnight slot.
In the back of every book, you see, there's a little
envelope, and in this little envelope, there's a little
card, and on that little card...*the little date the book is
due.*

(Holds up stamper) This is my stamper. Oh yes,
I wasn't letting them keep this. It's lovely— It
contains every date there ever was. You don't
believe me? *(Closes eyes, fiddles with stamper dials)*
"August 27, 1883,"...there, that's the date Mount
Perboewaten explodes in Krakatoa, thirty-six
thousand people perish under the ash. It's all in
here! All the trials and joys of history. *(Closes eyes,
fiddles with dials)* "January 25, 1971"...oh, January
25, 1971...Helen...Shattock is walking her dog in
Dayton, Ohio when a frozen block of urine from
the lavatory of a Pan Am jet, falls, and hits her on
the head, killing her instantly. Mind you, *(Fiddles
with stamper)* same date, "1836", Cetewayo, King of

the Zulus, is born! Oh yes, this stamper contains
every birth in this room, not just Cetewayo's.
And death. Yes, our deaths too...somewhere...
My death is in here...somewhere...I just don't
know...where.... Still. Gives you a bit of respect
for it, doesn't it. The stamper.

So. Yes. So, each and every day I woke up, took
the bus, no, no wife, no children, I lived alone,
got to the bibliotheque, put my labeled lunch in
the employees icebox, gave a but-just-perceptible
nod to Brody van Brummelen, works in reference
fine fellow I'm sure except that I'm sure that
he's not and always angling for that acquisitions
position that by all rights is mine, I'm the next
in line! ...em, arrived at my desk, yes that's next,
quieted the patrons, "ssh" and advanced the date
on my little stamper...one notch.

Now listen, the overnight slot is strictly for those
books *not overdue*. But we checked anyway. That
was my job. To check. Now and then you'd find
a book a day or two overdue. Sometimes a week.
Once, a book was returned, in the *slot* mind you,
three months overdue—well we got over it, but
we weren't amused. And neither was the violator
when he saw the fine ho ho. Still. We'll proceed.

One morning... *(He writes "1986" on the chalkboard.)*
...one fine and miserable and typical morning,
nothing to give an inkling of what was to come—
(Significantly) I found this book in the pile.
*(He takes out a battered book from the box with a
tag attached to it labeled "Evidence #1".)* We'll label
it Eveydence #1. It is a Baedeker's travel guide,
in deplorable condition. Well, I was just about to

give the little card my stamp with the old stamper when my eyes suddenly sprang out of my head and rolled about on the floor and under the table. And why? Because I saw that this book was checked out in *1873* and no...no—never returned til it was returned. Do you understand? *(He writes "1873" on the chalkboard, and demonstrates the math.)* That's one-hundred-and-thirteen years....overdue! Astounded out of my wits I was. It must have been the great great grandson returning the book, a blot on the family only now being remedied. And returned in the overnight slot no less! Appalling. If you have a book one-hundred-and-thirteen years overdue...you go to the counter, you admit your lapse, you pay the fine. Well, whoever it was, he wasn't getting away with it, not a chance, I checked the files—oh yes, we keep all the files, and I found the page and here it is. *(Takes out a page from a ledger labeled)* "Eveydence #2." *(Reads)* "Baedeker's Travel Guide, checked out November 12th, 1873 by capital A...period." *(Writes "A." on chalkboard)* That's the name. Capital A. Period. About as vague as they come, but never mind, what's his address, so I can send him the fine of his life. *(Reads)* "Post Office Box 121, Dingtao."

Well Dingtao didn't ring any bells so I got out the old Atlas. *(He procures an Atlas and pages through it.)* I've always liked Atlases. They allow you to travel all over the world—*without the expense.* Yes, it's true, I had never left Holland. I had rarely left Hoofddorp. I went to Gouda once to see how they made the cheese. But the tour wasn't given that day, I don't know why, so never mind. Here it is,

Dingtao, near Kaifeng. And no, it seems Kaifeng is not near Hoofddorp. No. Nor Rotterdam. No. It's China! Now how a Chinaman managed to check out a book from a Dutch library without a residence in the Netherlands, well—that would be the first of many puzzlers in this twisty mystery of a tale. And was he even a Chinaman? After all, the notes scrawled in the margins of the book were written in every language under the sun. Including Welsh. Well, it was none of my business. I filled out the standard form notifying our man of the pretty fine awaiting him, and bunged it off to China, and that was that.

But was that really that? No. That was not in any way...that. I couldn't get the miscreant out of my mind. I didn't reshelve the book, no, I thumbed through it. I took it home with me. I carried it about. And one day as I was flipping through it, I came upon this. *(Pulls from book)* Eveydence #3. Bookmark. But not just any bookmark. No. A bookmark *by proxy*. An unredeemed claim ticket for one pair of trousers left in a Chinese Laundering establishment. Oh, in China? No. In London. In *(Writes on chalkboard) 1913*, seventy-three years previous.

Well. My life went on, the bus, the books, the "how are you today, Brody," and "no, I don't believe my lunch is taking up too much room in the icebox, Brody, no, well, I'm sorry you feel that way," and the organizing of the cart and a "have a good night yourself" and then off with the lights and home again, but I'll say this...I got to thinking about those trousers. In fact, I couldn't *stop*

thinking about those trousers. In fact I had more
than one *dream* about those trousers, Trousers,
Trousers, Trousers, Trousers until I couldn't take
it anymore. Never claimed! Oh sure, the shop
probably went defunct years ago, but perhaps...
not. But of course, what was I going to do—
fritter away my vacation days just to go to London
for some non-existent trousers? Hah, I don't think
so. No. On the contrary. *(Beat)* I *applied* to travel to
London on *library business. (Eagerly)* To claim the
trousers you see on behalf of the library to recoup
some of the losses the library would no doubt
accrue from the unpaid fine. It was, perhaps, the
most daring gambit I had ever devised, but I felt
I was on solid ground, and what do you know,
the application was...rejected. Flat out. With a
reprimand attached about "frivolous requests."
Oh I was beside myself and I did a bit of
inconspicuous sulking, and then a bit of
conspicuous sulking and then I was calm again.
But damn it to hell, I still couldn't get the pants
out of my head, so I went to London all the same....

(We hear the thirties tune, Life Begins at Oxford
Circus, *or similarly jaunty thirties-vintage tune
from an English "sweet" band.)*

...expending...precious...vacation...time.

(And we see slides of London as—)

London. Dear God the chaos! The bustle! Oh this
was a terrible mistake, why wasn't I home in
Hoofddorp in front of the goggle box, cup of tea,
nothing ever on but I didn't mind, tall red buses
and sweet shops run by Pakistanis—and not very

good sweets at that—and the Bloody Tower and the Roman Wall and to think this all used to be swamps and mastodons. "What's this? Something for the French tourist—*Les Misérables*? That looks interesting—"the miserable"—"It's all about me in London," I thought, and I had never seen a play before, so I paid, and it's true, after two hours, I was more "miserables" than I had ever been before. Still, we'll proceed.

To the Holloway Road and the Chinese Laundry and...well what do you know, it was still there. The shop. So I strode in, waved around my claim ticket, and I came out with a pair of trousers. *(From the box he extrudes—)* Eveydence #4. Trousers. And never cleaned in all that time because they were in such a state of disrepair to begin with. A common laundering policy apparently, to protect the shop from accusations of negligence, and I was all the gladder for it, because it meant that any clues would be left *in situ* as they say.

And I was rewarded. I checked the pockets and I found...this. *(Extrudes from pocket with evidence tag attached—)* A used tram ticket. Eveydence #5. From 1912. A tram that ran in Bonn. Ger-ma-ny.

(And we hear the tune Ungarwein *by von Geezy and his Orchestra, or similarly vaguely Germanic thirties-vintage upbeat and librarian-inspiring tune [a song by the Comedian Harmonists, e.g.] and see a slide of Bonn and the Municipal Transportation Headquarters.)*

Well I don't know what got into me, feverish,
I took a bus to Bonn, to the Municipal
Transportation Headquarters to read up on
Incident reports for the month of March 1912.
Oh yes, I was a regular detective now. It was a
shot in the dark, I know, but I figured any scofflaw
making loose with library rules might have made
some trouble on a tram in Bonn as well. Well you
never know. And hey ho, this is what I found.
(Takes out from his box—) A photeystat I'll label #6,
and reads, in the German, as written by the tram
conductor, as follows—*"Ein Mann mit einem Bart
und einem neu"*— *(Stops short, to audience—)*
Sprechen sie—oh, no, yes of course...em, let's see...
(And he translates—) "A man with beard and
curious hat and smelling truly foul, boarded
the tram at Potsdamer Platz with a mangy dog.
Although there were plenty of seats, he *refused
to sit,* and instead paced up and down the aisle
with his dog distracting the other passengers
and myself. A dirty Jew, I threw him off at
Wittlesbach."

Well, surely this wasn't the same man as the man
who owned these trousers, but there was a chance,
slim, and I was hooked. And I hated it! What was I
doing in Bonn!? —There's always something about
German food that gives me— *(He's said too much
and now it's too late.)* —well it gives me flatus...
(More awkwardness) ...wind... *(Unjustifiably peevish
toward audience)* ...and why that's any conern of
yours I have no idea.... *(Quickly turning to
Baedeker's to change the subject)* Bonn, devastated
by the Normans, rebuilt, devastated by Frederick
III, rebuilt, devastated yet again in World War

II...rebuilt! In a chocolate shop I knocked over
an enormous display of marzipan and by the end
of the day, it was...rebuilt. Moved to tears by the
humanity of it all. The persistence, the forbearance.
Or I would have been, if "A Period" hadn't kept
doing the backstroke across my brain, who is he!
No no, I needed a distraction. Quick—I ducked
into a playhouse, showing a play called *(Perplexed
and dismayed) ...Les Misérables*. It was exactly the
same. Only worse. And it was no distraction!—
The tram, the trousers, the travel guide, I had to
find out more about this man. But how? A dead
end it seemed. "Curious hat" "smelling foul"
"threw him off at Wittlesbach". Hang on. What's
that about a dog. *(Draws a dog on the chalkboard)*
He had a dog, it said, in Germany, in 1912. And he
was in England in *1913* long enough to drop off his
trousers. But! For the past hundred years, there's
been a law in England—all dogs from foreign
countries must be put in quarantine *(Draws prison
cell around dog)* for six months on the grounds
of Rabies Prevention, there being no rabies in
England. Could it be then that our man was forced
to leave his dog in English quarantine? Because,
if so, there would be records! I called in to
Hoofddorp extending my vacation, ignored the
grumblings on the other end, worried a little about
giving Brody the one-up but I'd attend to that,
and like a shot, I was back on British soil, rifling
through files for dogs deposited between March
1912 and November 1913, and here was something
very curious—only one dog, stay with me here,
one dog alone, was put in quarantine during that
period, who, after six months, was not reclaimed.

That dog's name was... *(Writes on chalkboard)* ...Sabrina....

(We hear a scratchy recording of It's a Long Way to Tipperary *[preferably by John McCormack] or similar first World War vintage war song, and see a slide of soldiers in trenches.)*

Sabrina. October 1914 and Sabrina still not claimed. World War I had started by then, ten million men would be slaughtered by the end, and the German dog, Sabrina, she too was put down, at last.... Gassed... And as I stood there in that office, I began to wonder... *(Looks about)* What was I doing here?! But! And yet! What was that dog doing here. And what was anybody doing in those trenches in 1914— *(To slide of soldier)* —oh but you doughboys had a song for that, didn't you, how did it go— *(Sings waveringly, but jauntily, the old soldier song [to tune of* Auld Lang Syne*]—)* "We're here because we're here because we're here because we're here...." Yes, well enough of that.

The veterinarian's report on Sabrina is a tearjerker and reads in part— *(Reading scrap of paper with Evidence label dangling on it)* "This dog was brought to us with its footpads torn to shreds. And yet, when we told the dog to sit, it whined and whimpered, and refused to sit, and cowered in terror, as if sitting would bring with it a terrible beating." Poor Sabrina! And remember now, our man in the tram was reported as pacing up and down, *refusing to sit.* Well. This was getting interesting. Not riveting. But interesting. And nothing else of note except this, Except this!—

(Reveals, attached to the report, with its own evidence tag) —a release statement, handwritten by our Mister Mystery, oh yes, matching to a tee all the loops of the ells and ees that we have here in the margins of the bloody Baedekers! And he signed it—*"A" period.* And he wrote, "I give full authorization to these fellows to keep for the proscribed allotment of time, my dog, *Zebrina."* Not Sabrina. But "Ze." With a Z, E Zebrina. Well. "What sort of a name is that?" I wondered. So I looked it up in the dictionary, and encyclopedia, and one of those "name-the-baby" books and do you know what I found? Nothing. Still. I tucked it away in the back of the thinking thing that I cleverly carry around with me, sometimes, and there was this too—our man was required on this form to leave the name and address of a man in the Country who could vouch for him, and he wrote "the estate of the Lord of Derby, Attention: Thomas Wright."

And here's where things take a turn. And I'm talking about my stomach, for one. And here's why. I did a bit of research. Thomas Wright did live on the estate of the Lord of Derby but it was **almost two hundred years previous to the date of the Release Statement, Thomas Wright lived on the estate of the Lord of Derby from 1720 to 1754.** 1754. Two hundred and thirty-two years before the Baedeker's book was returned. Well this didn't make any sense. I was a bit scared now...no one lives that long...surely...surely he wrote down the first name that came to his head, having no one truly who could vouch for him in England.... Surely! But if you think I wasn't up in Derby the

next day, to the archives now overseen by the
National Trust, sifting through the account books
of Thomas Wright, well, you'd be wrong. This was
getting funny, and I didn't like it.

Eveydence #9. A page from Wright's Account
Book. Whose now? Thomas Wright's. He kept the
accounts of the estate of the Lord of Derby. How
many chamberpots ordered and whatnot. And a
diligent man was he. And good for us. And here's
why. Year, 1748. Page 112, line 8—"Earthstopper—
hired for week. Four pence." So what? So this—
in the margins next to the line, and on the back of
the page, Wright scribbled the following— (*And he
acts out the following in a clearly rehearsed, but rather
stiltedly rendered performance [though still managing
to impart an air of mystery to the "man in the funnel-
shaped hat".])*

> Whilst riding in coach, early evening,
> encountered a most curious man wearing
> faded yellow funnel-shaped hat roaming
> grounds of estate.
> "Sir," I said, "You are trespassing on private
> ground belonging to the Lord of Derby, you
> don't belong here."
> "I don't belong here, I don't belong anywhere
> at all, but I'm everywhere nonetheless and you
> can thank your Lord for that."
> "Do you have a grievance with my Lord?"
> "You don't know the half of it," he replied, in
> an accent impossible to place, but if I had to
> venture, I would say half-French, half...monkey.
> "May I ask how my Lord has grieved you, sir?"
> "You may ask, but I mayn't answer—I'm not

allowed to tell you how he has wronged me."
"Then how do you expect my Lord of Derby to
make amends," I said, rather exasperated. And
here, the curious man doubled over, and said
that was the funniest joke he had ever heard.
He said evidently we have been talking about
two different Lords. Well, obviously an escapee
from Bedlam, but suddenly remembering that
I was in desperate need of an earthstopper for
tomorrow's hunt, I took the liberty of asking
this crooked man if he would like a night's
employment. At the word "earthstopper,"
his eyes lit up.

Hold on. Stop the narrative. What's earthstopping.
Well, let's look it up. (*We see a slide of Joseph
Wright's nineteenth-century painting* The
Earthstopper.) Oh yes, here's a picture of it and a
faded miserable picture it is. Apparently it's a little
tactic developed by the foxhunting gentry. Foxes,
apparently, live in dens, snug little places.... At
night, the foxes leave their dens, and skulk about,
looking for supper. Otherwise, it's the dens for
them. Well, if you live on a big estate, and you're
throwing a foxhunting party in the morning,
you don't want all the foxes in their dens, no.
Your guests will say, one and all, "well that was
a lousy party." So what do you do. You employ
an *earthstopper*, who goes out with his lantern and
spade the night before, and while the fox is out,
he stops up his den right up to the top with earth.
When the fox returns, he can't find his home,
"what miserable earthstopper's done this," says
the fox, "burying my wife and all my lovelies, and
now I must roam the hills til morn and find a fix

to this conundrum". And, of course, in the morn—
while the fox is aroaming—the dogs, the horns,
the horses, the slaughter. Lovely. Now back to
the narrative.

> ...At the word "earthstopper," his eyes lit up.
> "Oh, are you one who appreciates a good hunt?"
> "Well no, I like the idea of the little fox roaming
> about with no place to return to—it's...funny."
> As he appeared exhausted I bade him ride in
> the coach, which he did, but he would not sit.
> When I insisted he sit, he insisted with equal
> force he would not. Unable to abide by a man
> who insists on standing stooped in front of me
> in a coach, I bade him walk on behind until....

And here the little anecdote suddenly and forever
stops, the next page missing, you see...Thomas
Wright, you see, grew liquidy in the mind, over
time, and the little children would steal in, and
steal his official papers to use for kites, and the
life of Wright got snagged in trees and down
drainpipes. *(With unexpected bitterness)* And whose
doesn't.

But! We have this. A man who wouldn't sit on a
coach, a man who wouldn't sit on a tram, a man's
dog who wouldn't sit in a kennel, a man with a
grievance against some lord, and a man with a
funny hat. Well. I'm no mathematician, but even
I could see that it was beginning to add up. *(Beat)*
Not that I was bad in mathematics, mind you.
Next to Rosa van der Werff, I was top in my class,
for a year. And that's where I met her actually.
Rosa. In math. Oh she had a wonderful brain
for...what are those things...variables. We'd do

our homework after school, that's how it started.
Fine old time though—giggling, of all things...
I wasn't even supposed to be in her class but I
was transferred over, heaven knows why...
(*Now intensely introspective*) ...there's a thought
for you.... (*And comes out of it when he notices the
audience*) Oh, yes, well enough of that, em, look
at this.

(*We see a slide projected—*)

This is a page from a fourteenth-century German
manuscript, depicting a man with a yellow funnel-
shaped hat. He's of the Hebraic faith. How do I
know? Because all men of the Hebraic faith had to
wear a funny hat just like this one. *In the fourteenth
century*, that is. All of this weighed heavily on
the mind as I returned to the day-to-day in
Hoofddorp. I stamped, oh yes, I filed, I fined,
but *inside* the brains were churning like the
machinery in a cheese factory. When it *isn't* closed.
I had clues, eveydence, but what did it mean?
The patrons were noisy, I didn't care, overdue
books came in, I didn't care, someone stole my
lunch from the icebox, I...cared, but not as much
as I would have.

And then, one day, *it happened*. I was manning the
information desk, when I received an urgent call,
ring ring, from a patron inquiring about the
amount of direct sunlight one should allow a
Zebra Plant. Well I got out the handy reference
guide to houseplants, turned to the index, looked
up Zebra Plant, and what do you think I saw right
below it? "Zebrina!" With a Z, E, as in the dog!
"Zebrina Pendula. Page 130." Surely it meant

absolutely nothing, but I flipped violently to the
page all the same and there at the top, (*And he
reads in his houseplant book—*) "Zebrina Pendula,
Latin for the common houseplant Tradescantia"...
and then...a shiver...for in parentheses..."also
known as...the Wandering Jew..."

I swallowed hard. For in a little-used musty
little corner of my head, I remembered hearing
something once about a myth of a Wandering Jew.
Oh Great Guns! In a flash I dashed to the card
catalog, "move out of my way, Brody," and
"damn it, Brody, this is *more* important," and
"oh wouldn't *you* like to know," and "scramoosh,
scramoosh, goodbye, scramoosh"...made sure
the coast was clear...went straight to the drawer
I needed, because I'm clever...*and found it.* (*And he
demonstrates a tattered library catalog card.*) *Tales of
the Wandering Jew.*

As the story goes, and it's been going for centuries,
there once was a cobbler, a Jew, kept to himself,
never married, stayed out of trouble, living in
Judea, around thirty-six anno domini, although
no one in the world knew it was thirty-six anno
domini...not knowing there was a *dominus* in their
midst to make it anno domini. And can you blame
them. Would *you* recognize a miracle if you saw
one? What if you think, "Oh, I'll never see a
miracle." Or what if you think, "well at least
I'm sure I haven't seen one yet." What if...you're
wrong?

It was April, hot day it was in Judea, the smells
of the Pesach meal the night before still lingering,
and he, our Jewish cobbler, at work with awl and

lace, in his little shop, on a shoe—when there was
a terrific shouting and haroo outside his window.
He went out on his front step and there on the
street, a procession of soldiers and convicted men
toting their crosses, no doubt to Golgotha. The
cobbler had seen it all before, and had little to say
about it—like I said, he minded his own affairs.
When suddenly, one of the frailest and sorriest of
the convicted lot collapsed, right there, right on the
steps, right by the door of our cobbler. The name
of the collapsed man was Yeshua, and he was a
mess. Well. "What do I do," thought the cobbler.
Underneath the lintel, he stood. The lintel. The top
of the doorframe. He stood under it. Yes? Good.
Underneath the lintel he stood. Not lentil...*lintel*.
You have to understand this or all is lost.
Underneath the lintel he stood, and tussled
with his quaking brain. "Let him lie on your
step a minute, let him catch his breath, it can do
no harm." But already the Roman soldiers were
pressing this Yeshua to get up, and telling the
cobbler to cease in this aiding and abetting or he'd
have to answer for it himself *with a cross of his own!*,
and the cobbler was shot through and through
with fear, he had a great fear of the law, you see,
and a greater fear of death, and his hand was
forced besides, and he thought, "I don't know this
Yeshua, he's probably a thief, a murderer even,
although he doesn't look like a murderer, but a
troublemaker no doubt," and this was trouble
the cobbler could do without, so the cobbler
says to this Yeshua, he says to this man with the
cross..."get off my step...go on...move on...enough
tarrying...do your resting somewhere else!"...

And this Yeshua did get up, calmly, and turned
to the cobbler and said— "I will go...but you,
you will tarry til I come again."

And off he went, and there we go, and the cobbler
didn't think twice about that little episode, and he
lived to be an old man and knew his end was near,
which was fine by him, by now he was sick of
living. He got ill...wrote out his will...and then...
he got well. Lived a few more years, got sick again,
called everyone to his bedside...and then...fie upon
it, he got well again. And then he began to notice
an even curiouser phenomenon. He noticed,
upon reaching the age of eighty, that instead of
appearing older, he was looking, well, younger.
And he suddenly got the urge to go for a walk,
and he left his house and was never seen by his
family again.

For fifty years he lived in this vagabond state,
incognito, getting younger all the while, and then,
he started to get older again, which went on for
fifty years, and then, younger again, and fifty
years of that, and on and on, older, younger, older,
younger. And by this time there was more than a
little groundswell claiming that this man Yeshua
with the cross was more than he seemed to be,
indeed...indeed, that he was the son of God...of all
things...and that He would come again at the end
of days as the long-awaited meshiach, and the
cobbler hearing these rumors began to put two
and two together, what was it that that Yeshua
said? "I will go, but you, you will tarry til I come
again." Holy Scamander, it all made sense to him
now. He was going to be stuck on this lousy old

earth until the Second Coming. "So there was a
God after all," he thought. Well that's Good. And
God had it in for *him* specifically. Not good. Bad.
Really awful. For over time, this Jew discovered
two stipulations of this unique curse which made
the thing more than unbearable. One—that he may
never rest. Physically impossible for him. That
means never sleep. Never lie down. Never sit
down. Never kneel. Could he lean? A little. But
just a little. So that's one stipulation, and not very
nice—I mean...sitting down...it's a wonderful
thing, a little rest, when you're exhausted, it isn't
asking much, and if you're not allowed to sit, you
become *beyond* exhausted, you just want to stop,
for a moment, and if you can't stop, then at least
crawl, on your knees, but if you're not allowed
to crawl, then you just want to die, and if you're
not allowed to die.... It's grisly. But Number Two
Stipulation is just as worse, in a way, and it's this—
the Jew *can never identify himself.* He is never
allowed to confirm his own existence to his fellow
man. He can be nothing more than a myth,
whether he's a myth or not.

Now then. Let's get one thing absolutely clear.
The Wandering Jew *is* a myth. Not the houseplant,
mind you. No—

(We see a slide of houseplant.)

—this is a picture of the houseplant, and as you
can see, the tendrils are, shall we say, wandering,
from the pot, yes, and so it became known as the
Wandering Jew. And this is a picture of it. And
it's mine. A documented photeygraph of the
Wandering Jew Zebrina Pendula houseplant.

I do not have a documented photeygraph of
the Wandering Jew *Jew*. Everyone knows after all
that it's just a myth. A myth. As in God is a myth.
As in that old myth that life has any meaning or
significance. A myth. But more and more I was
becoming convinced that although the Wandering
Jew was just a myth, I was in possession...of that
myth's...*pants*.

The woman on hold...waiting to hear about
her Zebra Plant...was, regrettably, forgotten,
completely. That is, until the next day when she
sent a letter of complaint to my superiors—I, who
had never received a complaint in my life! Oh it
made dear Brody's month, I don't know how he
found out about it. He even gave me a chocolate
for consolation. *(Steeped in bitterness)* I didn't need
his chocolate. *(Clarifying)* I ate it, but I didn't need
it. So yes...yes...it was becoming clear that this
overdue book was beginning to interfere...with my
work.... And yet I couldn't stop thinking about it!

Because...what if he *did* exist...I mean, a man
(Perhaps draws a man on the chalkboard) living
immortally, incognito, somewhere on this earth,
well that's odd enough, but if he existed, it meant
something even odder existed too...God...*God*....
And all the irate Zebra Plant owners and reference
department rivals in the world suddenly seemed...
a little less important than they did before...I used
to lose sleep over them.... Now I lost sleep over
something else.... Mister A period. Oh yes, I forgot
to mention another confounding coincidence—
that in more than one source, the name of the
Wandering Jew is *Ahasuerus*, do you see?

Ahasuerus. As in "please initial the rental
contract here, here and here Mister Ahasuerus."
"Righteeo— A period, A period...*A Period!*"

Well. I got to thinking. If I were in such a
predicament, in which a superior had foisted
an unreasonable condition upon me, well there's
two ways you can go, either (A) accept your new
condition grovelingly, or (B) find a way around it.
I've always been more of the option (A) sort of
man, it's nothing to be ashamed of—*but*—what
if you've been practicing option (A) for over a
thousand years, and now you're getting *a little
weary of it*? A superior makes an unreasonable
demand—in this case—your life, your history,
your trials and suffering, can never be
authenticated, or even communicated, no, no,
after a thousand years, option (B) begins to look
better and better—*find a way around it*. Trousers,
claim tickets, incident reports—what if these
things weren't as incidental, as accidental,
or casual and trivial as they *seemed*. Just
hypothetically speaking, if *you* were the
hypothetical Wandering Jew, wouldn't *you* drop
little clues, from time to time, nothing overt mind
you, nothing to catch His notice, but just little
things...like...oh, I don't know... conveniently
leaving your *pants*, for instance.... Or taking out
a discreet post office box in China.

(Slaps hand to forehead)

China! Of course! The man has a post office box
in China! If I really wanted to settle this once and
for all, be done with this nonsense, all I had to do
was go to China. But! I mean...China...that seemed

just a little bit further away than, say...Neptune.
(Drawing a brain on the chalkboard) I put my brain
under some good hard scrutiny—it had been
playing fast and loose for too long and it needed
an audit. *(Speaks to drawing—)* "Brain! What in
heaven's name are you doing to me? Do you truly
believe that this mysterious man is—" "No!" says
the brain, "certainly not...or...oh...I don't know
anymore...."

...thus spoke the brain...thus began the beginning
of the end...because I felt myself more and more
believing...I who had never believed anything in
my life! *Accepted,* oh yes, I accepted plenty. But the
act of *accepting* and the act of *believing* are two very
different things. What was happening to me now,
was a very different thing indeed.... A book drops
into my lap one morning. Was it just an overdue
book...or a *challenge*.... Would *I* recognize a miracle
if I saw one...? And yet No, this was mad mad mad
mad mad. Back to my desk, stamp stamp away,
turn the notch one each day and forget about it.
What was I going to do, spend all my money to go
to China! I, who had Hunan Chicken, once, Once!
...and got the runs for a week! ...And there was this
too...my superiors wouldn't look kindly at any
more gallivanting any time soon. The overnight
slot was still clogged with piled-up books, and
even though I had plenty of vacation time left, I
was forced to sit if I had any desire to keep my job.

And so...I got ill. Oh yes, a cough, a sneeze, a
swoon, and I was sent home. But... *(Confiding)*
...it was all a ruse! I wasn't sick at all, no!, but I
had a week of sick leave to show for it! Oh clever

librarian—had anybody ever thought of that
before—*pretend* you're sick to get out of work—
no, I don't think so, that's a new one in the books
I bet.... Well I took the plunge... *(Now realizing
the weight of what he's done)* ...now take the leap...
absurd, but no choice, it was off with you...
to the land of rice, the Great Wall, and...rice.

*(We hear some chinoiserie number of a 1920s/30s
vintage, e.g.,* Limehouse Blues *[preferably by Ambrose
and his Orchestra], and see a slide of an overcrowded
Chinese city.)*

China! A billion people. In Beijing less than a day
and I believed it. At least a billion. And yet, it's
funny, I think the death of even a cricket is noticed
because as far as I could tell, they keep them all
in cages for pets. Back in Hoofddorp, a million
insects are caught in a million balls of lint behind a
million couches every day and dying and nobody
knows. Mind you, *(Fiddles with dials of stamper)*
in 1887 in Honan, China, a flood—like that!—
drownded three million people, three million! And
no one in Hoofddorp batted an eye at that either,
so the insects behind the couches shouldn't take
it personally, that's just the way it is. It may have
been three million and one people who drownded,
by the way, but what's that one to anyone but
that one. If it isn't someone you know, then it's all
just...behind the couch. Of course, if I snuffed it
tomorrow, would anyone notice? Oh yes, plenty.
Or rather, a few. Or rather, Brody. But in two
hundred years, five hundred, ten thousand, will
anyone care that *he* perished? No. Or any of us
here? ...No. Lord Harry, we're all behind the

couch, mutely struggling with our lint...not a
cheery thought. Standing in Jaiseng Road in
Beijing surrounded by a billion other souls can
do that to your thoughts, a diversion was needed,
I tried to get tickets for a show in town called...
Les Misérables—yes, I like it, I admit it—but I was
mistakenly given tickets to the Peking Opera
instead, and I went, and...I liked that too...I didn't
know what was happening to me...I had heard that
travel broadened the mind but at this rate I would
need a sombrero soon. But on to Dingtao, where I
greased a palm, a very easy thing to do in Dingtao,
as if our man had foreseen it all, and I obtained
access to the Post Office Box of Mister A period.

Inside...was one letter... *(He takes letter from box
with great anticipation, then opens it, to great
disappointment.)* ...from me, informing him of
his pretty fine. *(Then spots another letter)* And one
letter, and one letter! dated January 6th, 1906,
and here it is, Eveydence #11, written to our
man by one Esther Gelfer. In Yiddish. And of all
things...a love letter. An excerpt of which reads as
follows— "If you must know...I am in love with
you. Hopelessly. You probably don't remember
me, but I remember you. In our town of misery,
you suddenly appeared, and whistling that *funny
little song.*" Make a note of that. *(Draws a musical
note on the blackboard)* ..."I had never seen you in
Zabludow before that day two years ago, the day
the man with the phoneygraph came to get our
voices on that machine, but I was smitten—you
were shy, and knew every language under the sun,
and I invited you back to my embarrassing little
room. I was young, I was confused and you

gallantly refused to lie with me. You refused to
even sit down, in fact, and you left in a hurry, in a
sweat, nervously, endearingly, and left your jacket
behind. At any rate, I know you are well-traveled,
and I have emigrated to Amerikay and this is my
address and if ever you wish to reclaim your
jacket, it is here...and I am here,,,I am here...
Waiting...

*(He grunts, strangely moved by the letter. Pause. He
grunts again. The he snaps out of it and we see slide
with map of Zabludow and a slide of Polish protesters.)*

She must have left Zabludow after the Revolution
of 1905, Radical Jews in Russia and Congress
Poland joining Anti-Czarists demanding
democratic elections, and Czarist authorities
instigating pogroms to divert the masses...heads
chopped off to divert the masses...from their
heads, I suppose.... Well I couldn't stop now.
No time for fried rice, it was a slow boat to
Amerikay for me, to seek Esther Gelfer...out!

(And we hear Yiddisher Charleston *by the old
Gilt-Edged Four, or an appropriate klezmer tune of
1920s/30s vintage.)*

Well I got to New York. A slog and a half, but I did
it, I did it. Heart pounding, I looked up addresses,
made call after call, and at last do you know what
I found? That after being in New York for a year
and a month, Esther Gelfer moved. To Australia.
Shoot me through the eyes.

Well, feeling down, I thought about seeing a play
that night to cheer me up, a certain French musical,
but I took in a concert instead, outside, it was free

and what the heck, and then I went swing dancing,
of all things—there's a revival apparently— *(We
hear romantic swing music, and he gradually, haltingly,
rediscovers his feet)* —and I hadn't danced like that
since....well since...Rosa van der Werff was in my
arms in Hoofddorp too many years ago...oh I was
high as a kite that New York night, and I bored a
Japanese couple senseless explaining the Dewey
Decimal System while we shared a horse and
buggy through Central Park at midnight, oh it
was capital T Wonderful. I mean Thrilling. Both.
And. In the morning I shuffled over to the YIVO
Institute for Jewish Research and its Archives of
Sound Recordings and Photo Archives, oh yes, we
librarians know just where to go for the references,
and I unearthed this little item.

*(We see a slide of a shtetl in 1904 with ethnographic
surveyor with recording equipment.)*

Eveydence #13A—an ethnographic surveyor with
recording equipment in *Zabludow* in April, 1904.
And do you know who that is, that gentleman
to the left with his head just out of view?
(Significantly) Neither do I.

But! Eveydence #13B happens to be this—
*(Holds up a battered tape recorder [Preferably quite out
of date])* —a recording from an Edison cylinder—
(Also holds up an Edison cylinder) —one of the very
ones made on that Zabludow day. Now listen.

*(He plays tape, and we hear scratchy recording of
person speaking Yiddish, with whistling very faintly
in background.)*

That's Yiddish you're hearing, but listen harder.
Do you hear that? In the background? That...
whistling? What is that? Do you recognize it?
It isn't a Polish folk song, no, nor a Jewish one
neither, no. No, it's a little number entitled
When it's Nighttime in Italy— (Sings) "When it's
Nighttime in Italy, It's Wednesday over here,
When it's Fish Day in Germany, You can't get
shaved in Massachusetts" et cetera. First recorded
and released by Billy Jones and his Orchestra, in
New York in *April 1904! (Significantly)* And now
here it is being whistled by— *(Perhaps circling
drawing of man and the musical note)* —some
unidentified personage in a tiny remote shtetl in
Poland *the very same month*!? Well wouldn't it be
just like our well-traveled man, as Esther writes,
and I quote—to "whistle that funny little song"
in the background thus ensuring that he would
be recorded—incognito, but *in perpetuity*—that
he would *leave his mark*!

Well it was on to Australia!, find Gelfer, I had to.
And it was on the way, and only then, that I
remembered something.... I only had a week of
sick leave...and I had been gone.... *(Figures in head)*
a month and a half...I...was screwed. *(Disturbed)*
Still. We'll...proceed. We'll proceed.

(We see a slide of Australia.)

Australia, and what did I find. Dear Esther Gelfer.
Dead. For thirty-five years. And what did I expect?
A one-hundred-and-twenty-one year-old woman
to answer all my questions? Yes. I did find a chest
of Esther's effects *(Indicating suitcase of scraps)*,
there in the attic of her niece, now living outside

Brisbane. Dear...dead...Esther Gelfer, there I
stood..amongst the ephemera of your life. *(More
introspective)* There's a word. Ephemera. From
"ephemeral"—short lived—like those insects,
the ephemerids, *(Draws a mayfly on the chalkboard)*
mayflies living a day and all to find their perfect
mate, and then...die... *(He erases the mayfly.)*
...Esther Gelfer...never-married... Did you live
with regrets? "Settle down," you said to him.
"Settle down" you said to a man who might have
been the *Wandering Jew*, oh poor Esther...Cupid *is*
cruel...or just blind and ignorant.... What cruelty
isn't from blindness or ignorance...underneath the
lintel...a cobbler told a man with a cross to shove
on...and that made all the difference. *(Suddenly,
he seems overcome, voice cracking.)* ...Underneath
the lintel...underneath the lintel...it's supposed
to be an innocent place...where boys kiss their
sweethearts good night...in the first bloom of
love...Rosa Van der Werff...wearing those eyes
of hers... *(Weeps)* ...she *did* love me...she said
so...and what did I do? ...And what did I do?
...I must have been standing in an ice bucket—
blazing heart...cold feet... *(Pause)* ...and she married
another... *(Pause)* ...well you can't live with
regrets...how was I to know she was the one...
and only... *(Fighting tears and losing)* ...no, move
on...move on.... A...a...magician tells you to choose
any card in the deck, *(Increasingly bitter)* and so
with free will you do choose...but you don't realize
the magician has already subtly forced you to pick
the exact card he wanted you to pick. Magicians
call that a "Hobson's Choice." And in life we think
we make choices...but they're Hobson's Choices.

So who is this Hobson? Who is this magician gulling us? That's the question. Simply something named Chance? Or Fate? *(Looking up)* Or Something Else...

(Still fragile from breakdown) In the hope chest of Esther Gelfer— *(Pulls from box—)* a raggedy old jacket, and on the jacket, a faded yellow star, yes, like the type Jews were forced to wear in Augsburg *in the fifteenth century*, yes, and in the jacket—a coin. An old coin. A Roman coin, from the time of Tiberius. Issued? 37 A D. Eveydence? #16, underlined, circled, with exclamation points and arrows pointing to it!

(Emotionally) That night, outside Brisbane, I stared up at the stars until the old orbs watered—"how very...high they are..." ...Unreachable, that's the word..and a line from Job out of the blue blazed across the brain like a comet— "Hitherto shalt thou come...but no further..." But no, I'd have none of that talk. I was in for it now, Hobson knows I hadn't a choice, it was a world tour to track down this rapscallion, with the Baedeker's as my guide and clue-filled companion, for curse it all, if it's really him, then he's out there—he lives, he lives!

(We hear the jaunty Freilach Yidelach *by Dave Tarras [or a similarly spirited klezmer tune of 1920s/30s vintage by Tarras or Naftule Brandwein] as—)*

(Paging through Baedeker's, *looking at margins)* Let's see, he knows German, and Italian...so I went back to Germany, then Italy, then all over the world, where I found graffiti written in every

language, including Welsh, and saying especially this— *(Writes on board or wall)* "I Was Here."

(We see slides of Acropolis and bathroom stall.)

To Greece, then France, and I found the words on the side of the Acropolis, and in a bathroom stall in the Paris Metro, "I was here," "I was here"—

(We see slides of Norwegian coast, totem pole, Mayan temple, etc.)

—on a rock in Norway, on a totem pole near Juneau, on the thirty-first step of a Mayan temple in Uxmal...on a park bench in Stamford, Connecticut, on a statue on Easter Island... "I was here," "I was here," "I was here," *(Perhaps writes on wall)* "I was here.."!

(Music out. Pause. And calmly—)

But you might say... "Yes, but look here... those words could have been written by anyone. Perhaps you're not looking for the Wandering Jew at all, but Kilroy." And I would say to that... *(Searches for an answer and finally flipping the bird with both hands at the audience, in exasperation)* ...Fuck you! *(Then sincerely shocked at his behavior—)* And then I would apologize *profusely*, and dig about in my box of scraps for some more tangible proof.... *(Thinks, eyes light up, and pulls from box, now a little uncomfortably frantic)* ...Ah! Oh hoh! Look at this! Now look at this, look at this... Ripped from the Baedeker's...I took it from the Baedeker's... *(He holds up scrap with label dangling from it.)* ...an illustration of the ruins in Rome. But by now I was learning to shift my focus, follow the blur in the periphery, look in the margins, the

fringes, for that's where our man and The Truth
have set up shop. So I peered very closely at the
illustration of the ruins, and there in the corner,
very small, a drawing of moths, for flavor....

*(We see series of slides of the illustration, zooming
in until we see the moths, with words on the wing,
backwards—as if an impression from the page opposite.)*

...but look at the wings—there's words on them,
a ghostly vestige—they must have come from the
page opposite, from years of the two pages being
pressed together—you see? Yes? Yes? Yes? —But
no! The words don't correspond, so we can only
assume that at one point a piece of paper had been
inserted *between* the pages, and there was!, and
I tracked it down!, and it's this!—a theatrical
programme! Eveydence #77, from the year 1777!,
in *Holland*, for a performance entitled "The
Wandering... *(Reads surprised and profoundly
deflated)* ...Minstrel"? *(Beat)* "Minstrel"? No.
This said "Jew." This said "Jew." *(Stares at
paper in disbelief)* I swear to you, it was Jew. It said
Wandering Jew, I saw it.... *(Now quite lost on the stage,
he reads, softly to self, working hard to help himself
make sense of this setback.)* ..."Wandering Minstrel"...
(Then—) ...Mind you...there's a smoked herring...
called a red herring...that was used at one time to
lay trails to train hunting dogs, so the dogs could
learn to track the *aforementioned earthstopped fox.*
Well. For *advanced* training, the red herring was
used to *divert* the dog from the trail. All very
confusing for the dog but there's solace in this—
a herring may have been a false herring, but every
false herring still *had its purpose. (Perhaps looking at*

scrap then heavenward) There's never an accidental herring, oh no, every red herring, every digression, is a step, perhaps a step sideways or backwards, but it keeps you moving nonetheless... *(Softly, perhaps realizing for first time)* ...and there's joy...too...in that....

Yes...yes, I was back in *Holland* to dig this one up. Strode into the Hoofddorp library, as if I hadn't been gone a day, Brody was head of acquisitions now, "congratulations," I almost felt sorry for him, chained to a desk all the day as he was. And after a few gawping stares from the library patrons, and some rather unkind remarks about the hum wafting off my unwashed self, I was called into the offices of my superiors and told...to shove on. *(Humbled)* It was quite a blow. "...oh...well...oh... all right then...but what about my pension," I said. "Nothing doing," they said. "But....but then how will I manage? How will I enjoy a well-earned rest in my waning days?" "You won't. We're striking your name from the files, it will be as if...you were never here at all..." And I was shown out. And there on the steps, eating my chocolate from Brody, I stared in a daze from the other side of the door. At my old haunt, my second home. Underneath the lintel I stood, grappling with a thought. Yes? Should I? No?...Yes! And I marched back in, strode straight to my desk, stole my stamper, got out the sharpest letter opener I could find, and carved deep and irrevocably into my former desk so no one could ever be mistaken, "I WAS HERE....I WAS HERE." And then, oh boy did I run away, but fast.

Fine... *(Significance of losing job sinking in a bit)*
...fine, I lost my job.... *(Now more desperate)* I lost
my job... *(And full enormity hitting him)* I lost my
job... *(Clutches stamper, spluttering)* ...but I had the
history of man in my hand, and, and, *(Desperately)*
I have this.... *(And pulls from box an old horse brush
[or some other antique worthless object])* This...is...
a brush. *(Stares at thing with ever-growing
incomprehension)* Still. We'll proceed.

*(More desperately, he pulls from box, an acorn-sized
item in small pouch with label attached—)* Ah! Look
at this...look at this...this...now look at this...this
this may *look* small and insignificant, but it is
actually...the fossilized excrement of an ancient
turtle. Oh yes. And you may ask, "what does this
have to do...with the Wandering...Jew..." *(Long
pause, as he stares at fossilized excrement. Looks all
about the stage as if quite lost. All confidence in his
scraps has now left him, and he says, softly)* I don't
know...I don't know...I don't know...gone...gone
the turtle goes...but leaves a testament more
enduring than any of us can hope for... *(To
excrement/audience)* ...Do you know how Aeschylus
died, that towering playwright of ancient Greece?
It has to do with turtles. Apparently eagles pick
up turtles and carry them aloft until they find a
suitable rock to drop them on, to crack them open.
One day, an eagle thought Aeschylus' bald
head...was a rock. Exit Aeschylus. And if you think
"oh dear that's an awfully trivial death for such
a grand person," not to worry—fourteen people
in America die every year by vending machines
falling on top of them. Vending machines—
after shaking them for the fifty cents they just

devoured.... Life...fifty cents... *(Bitterly despairing)*
And it's not just the trivial deaths, no—all death
has a way of making one's life, no matter how
grand, seem silly and small—it's as if, as if
Life were Beethoven's *Ninth*, but instead of
culminating with a choir, a hundred-strong,
it culminates with..the squeak of a dog toy.
*(Becoming increasingly agitated, bewildered, intensely
bitter and tearful)* No, no *Ode to Joy*, nothing
exalting, nothing exulting, just senselessness,
senselessness, nothing miraculous, just a
nuisance—Life, Love, Your One Love...your
one love... *(Pause)* ...send her away...a mistake...
too late...carry on as if it didn't matter.... It did....
It *did*...but now it doesn't...for who can hear you,
in no time at all you're shunted off yourself and
there you go—all's forgiven, if only because...all's
forgotten...I used to be a librarian...what have I
done...I don't know... "To prove one life, and
justify another..."...with scraps...I'm sorry...I'm
sorry...I'm sorry.... *(He begins putting scraps back
in the box, and packing up, when suddenly he sees the
world's fair recording in the box [either a shellac disc or
a cassette purporting to be a recording from the record],
picks it up, perplexed.)* ...and yet...to say...or yell
out...or carve in a wall, if but once..."*I was here*..."
...well, there's this—last scrap, I promise....

*(And we see a slide of the World's Fair, and of the time
capsule exhibit.)*

At the 1939 World's Fair, in Queens, New York,
a time capsule was lowered, preserving all sorts
of artifacts in a shell of titanium, to be unearthed
a thousand years hence, a declamation of our little

existence in the twentieth century....Was our man
there, being attracted to such a notion? *(Pointing to
photograph)* Is he somewhere in this crowd? Hard
to say. But. There was a little booth at the Fair
where you could make a record of yourself...
for fifty cents. A few were left unclaimed. This
(Holding up tape or record) is a recording of one of
them.

*(And we hear a scratchy, and eerie, recording of an old
man, perhaps slightly reminiscent of* THE LIBRARIAN.
THE LIBRARIAN *echoing [with the beginning of
epiphany] in a whisper "and yet..." at same time as
voice in recording—)*

RECORDING: I am here...I am here...at the World's
Fair.... Is it?... Is the world fair?... Hardly... And
yet...I'll say this...to any who can hear...I am here...
I am here...I am here...I am here...I am here....

*(And as the recording continues with numerous "I am
here"s,* THE LIBRARIAN, *overlapping, sings slowly and
softly, his eyes lighting up as a much-desired realization
sinks in—.)*

"We're here because we're here because we're here
because we're...here..."

*(The recording fades out, and with a sort of beatific
grin—)*

You don't have to believe me...Say I made it all
up... "He made it all up," I don't care anymore....
I'm tired.... Yes, I'm tired...but *I'm not stopping my
pursuit neither*...no.... And why? Because I don't
think Mister A Period has stopped, no, not given
in, No, and never will. And if one day He Above
tells our man, at last, that he may lie down...he'll

sit. "Sit then", he'll stand. "Stand then", he'll *walk*.
(God increasingly angry/exasperated) "Walk then,"
he'll dance. On principle. No, no repentance—
no, for in the greatest act of defiance known to
humankind, our man *will* find a way, this I know,
mark my words, to behold this hash of a creation,
to take this muck and holy mess of a life, and
winnow out and revel in every bit of beauty and
worth that's in it so long as he's in it, so there. And
so. We Shall Proceed. Although...the trail trails off.
The last promising sighting of him was over fifty
years ago—testimony of a fellow doing a sort of
buck dance outside the fences at Buchenwald....
"The doomed souls within were probably
delirious," you'll say...and what did they see
after all but a ragged Jew on the other side of the
camp fence.... *But, you see, our man lives incognito.*
He could be there everywhere you look, but you
won't see him.... If in Mexico, in a sombrero he'll
be. A kimono in Kyoto, a thong in New Guinea,
wooden clogs in Zander aan Zee... And I'll be
following just behind him.... And after all these
years, both of us...beginning to learn...to *dance*....

(Up on the Yiddish tune Zetz *by Annie Lubin
[or some spirited klezmer tune or Yiddish song from
the 1920s/30s] as he exits the stage, with the
Baedeker's in his hand)*

END OF PLAY

AFTERWORD

A spot of grocery shopping, a few diapers changed, dinner, a chat on the phone, a shower, a shave, and an arduous mission retrieving a small round dog toy from under the couch—that has been my day today, and all in all, little to write home about, certainly nothing demanding deep consideration, nothing out of the ordinary, nothing strange. That is, if it weren't for three incontrovertible Facts:

1) The universe contains well over 500,000,000,000 galaxies, with each galaxy containing over 1,000,000,000,000 stars, of which our vast, blazing and life-bestowing sun...is one.

2) The Earth is 4,600,000,000 years old, in which time, from the Pre-Cambrian Era to the Present, a dizzying, terrifying number of inhabitants—amoebas and trilobites, dust mites and Neanderthals—have all struggled to live from one hour to the next. (Indeed, more living creatures are in my stomach (and yours) at this moment than the total number of human beings that have ever existed.)

3) I will die. I will be dead in sixty years, though it's entirely conceivable that I'll be dead before the week is out.

And suddenly all the props holding up my warm
and secure little existence are kicked away and
used for kindling. The imagination is taxed to
exhaustion and left numb and agape when it even
begins to fathom the implications of these Facts.
They beggar the most breathless hyperbole.
Three simple Facts, three confirmed and
undeniable Facts—the immensity of the universe,
the incomprehensibly vast history of the Earth,
and our inescapable mortality—loom over all
of us like three paisley mastodons. When I shine
these three Facts upon any moment in my life,
suddenly nothing, absolutely nothing, isn't
strange, bewildering, and out of all whooping.
These Facts turn every memorable or trivial or
utterly forgettable moment of my existence—
shopping, eating trout with spouse, lying prostrate
retrieving dog toy—into the Apotheosis of the
Comic and Tragic, the Inconsequential and
Crucial, the Banal and Profound. These Facts loom
so large, in fact, that they are rather easily ignored.
Three paisley mastodons get up with us in the
morning and sleep with us at night but, for the
most part, they're very quiet pachyderms, and
consequently, amazingly, they blur into the
unimportant background, even though one day,
with trumpeting bellows, they will trample me
into oblivion. Time and again I explain to myself
that these Facts are interesting, profound even,
but not pertinent to my daily life. NO. In truth,
everything else is but shadow compared to these
Facts. They are the trump cards to all the ordinary
cards I hold in my hand and call "my life."

I write plays to help me keep these Three Facts in the front of my head. In other words, I write to try to keep myself engaged with the Bewildering and Infinite. But why did I write UNDERNEATH THE LINTEL in particular?

All my plays are first inspired by music, and UNDERNEATH THE LINTEL was inspired particularly by certain klezmer/yiddish music from the 1920s (and earlier). The "jaunty melancholy," the "dancing-despite-it-all" quality it contained, the defiance even—a certain "finding-joy-despite-all-the-evidence-to-the-contrary" quality in the music—compelled me to try to express it as a play.

In 1976, in Laetoli, in Tanzania, some members of Mary Leakey's archaeology team were throwing chunks of dried elephant dung at each other, (as archaeologists are wont to do in their free time). When one of the paleontologists dove to the ground to avoid being pelted by dung, he noticed fossilized footprints of an animal, left in hardened volcanic ash from 3.8 million years ago. After two years of excavation, all number of animal prints were discovered, including, unexpectedly, unmistakably, the footprints of hominids— our ancient australopithecine ancestors. The fact that these prints were preserved—prints by an anonymous ancestor going about a no doubt everyday activity—testifies to me of the great Conundrum of History: What is saved, and what is lost?

There used to be a sequence in UNDERNEATH THE LINTEL which I considered and then excised

before the New York production. After the
Librarian points out the words on the moth's
wing, and calls them a "ghostly vestige," he
mentions how "vestige" comes from the Latin
word "vestigium", meaning "footprint." The
Librarian then alludes to the footprints left by
our ancestors in Laetoli, and (unbeknownst to
the Librarian) we see a slide of those Laetoli
footprints, and then a subsequent 15-second
slideshow depicting the subsequent 4-million
year history of Humankind, full of our best and
worst, and ending with a picture of a footprint
left by the first man on the moon.

I loved the idea, and it looked really horrible when
we actually tried to execute it, and then I hated the
idea. So the sequence is out. But hopefully the idea
can still be found in the play. "Still, we'll proceed,"
the Librarian says over and again, somehow we'll
proceed, we haven't a choice, and perhaps such a
sentiment has somehow driven the evolution of
humanity itself, in tiny steps. Oh yes, we'll often
go sideways or backwards, but continue we will,
and perhaps "there is joy, too, in that."

What, after all, do we do with the fact that
suffering has dogged humanity (and certainly not
just humanity, but the 3 billion-odd species that
have populated this planet) every step of the way?
Calculated cruelty as well as utterly random
events—10 million die in the senselessness of
W W I and a woman is struck down by a frozen
block of urine. The fact that we die is a great
fat conundrum, and it will continue to be a
conundrum for me until...well until I die. What

does my little life mean when set against the huge
backdrop of human history? And what's human
history set against the ridiculously unimaginable
backdrop of the history of the universe? (At the
Rose Planetarium in New York, there's a walk
representing the history of the observable universe
and at the end of the walk, there's a single hair,
representing the 50,000 years of human existence.)
And what do we do with the fact that because we
only live our lives once, a single event, or a single
mistake, can send our lives into a wholly
unanticipated and undesired direction?

The first performance of UNDERNEATH
THE LINTEL in New York was scheduled for
September 18, 2001. The Soho Playhouse, being
in Soho, was inaccessible for a week after the 11th,
but we invited the neighborhood to see the show
on the 19th. Yet although the events of 9/11 were
singular and tragic, they were not, unfortunately,
so out of the ordinary, when one considers the
whole of history. On September 11, people were
murdered out of anger and ignorance, victims who
didn't want to die, and weren't expecting to die
just then. Considered in this light, such events
occur on larger and smaller scales every day,
and have been occurring every day for thousands
of years.

So it was while I was listening to the klezmer
music, and trying to think of a dramatic structure
that would allow me to encompass a lot of history
(in lieu of the Three Facts), that I remembered
the story of the Wandering Jew. Now I was quite
aware that the myth of the Wandering Jew was

originally an anti-Semitic tale, but the myth had
taken on more complex meanings in its 700-odd
year history, and I felt, besides, that an artist can
always appropriate myths for his own ends.

(I would later discover that a film made in Yiddish
by Jews in the early 1930s called *The Wandering Jew*
was made to warn a generally ignorant world
of the growing Nazi menace. In the film, the
Wandering Jew is depicted as a noble figure,
bearing witness to history. I've received letters
calling UNDERNEATH THE LINTEL anti-Semitic
and other letters calling it "anti-Christian" [for the
portrayal of a cruel Christ]. That said, I've also
received letters calling the play too "pro-Zionist".
So hey ho.)

In a sense, despite the Wandering Jew's
seemingly unique situation, his predicament is the
predicament of all humanity—he made a mistake,
a single mistake "underneath the lintel", when
he put fear and self-interest ahead of compassion.
Everyone does it all the time. And he was forced to
live with that mistake the rest of his days. Did the
punishment fit the crime? No. But that's often true
of punishments and crimes. And even though he
was condemned to live for a near-eternity, the fact
that he is not allowed to be anything more than a
myth (by not being allowed to communicate his
existence to his fellow man) puts him in practically
the same spot as the rest of humanity; namely,
that his life means seemingly next-to-nothing in
the great scope of history.

However, he is a human being, and he isn't going
to give up so easily. Humanity inevitably finds the

strength, despite our mistakes and tragedies, to rebuild, to persevere, to proceed, until death does us in. Graffiti throughout the ages (in a Lascaux cave or on a New York subway train) testify to the fundamental human need to affirm our own existence to each other and to the Heavens. For our Librarian, the scraps left behind by the alleged Wandering Jew prove that he will never stop seeking "a way around" God's edict. And if the Wandering Jew has been condemned by God to witness thousands of years of human suffering, then almost in defiance, he will seek out all that is good and worthy and beautiful, and if he is forced to "walk", he'll do God one better and Dance. Which of course, God no doubt wanted all along. This is the defiance, sadness, and hope I found expressed so fully in the klezmer music I had been listening to.

The Librarian made a mistake underneath the lintel—sending the one girl he ever loved away. His ensuing, long-sublimated spiritual crisis feeds his determination to find meaning in the clues he uncovers.

But my point isn't that we should all believe in the Wandering Jew, or even in God, for that matter. Rather, anything at all—for the Librarian it was an impossibly overdue book—can be an invitation to the miraculous. And also this: That in the face of overwhelming existential bewilderment and terrible suffering, to respond with a little defiant dancing (in all its myriad forms) is a very human and very wondrous thing.

On one end of a spectrum is Coincidence, on
the other end Profound Serendipity. The only
difference between the two is how much meaning
we choose to ascribe to a particular event. I'm still
working out where on the spectrum I should put
the following:

A few months back, I was paging through an
encyclopedia of philosophy when I came across
the word "Sublime," which is defined as "the
presence of transcendent vastness or greatness....
While in one aspect, it is apprehended and
grasped as a whole, it is felt as transcending our
normal standards of measurement.... It involves
a certain baffling of our faculty with feeling of
limitation akin to awe and veneration; as well as
a stimulation of our abilities and elevation of the
self in sympathy with its object."

The word sublime comes from "sub" (**under**) +
"limen" (which, like "limit", is a word derived
originally from..."**lintel**").

Though we rarely recognize the place, underneath
the lintel is where each of us stands every day,
every moment, of our life.

SLIDE LIST

Below is a list of the slides used in the
Off-Broadway production

4 slides of various London sites

1 slide of a building standing in for the Bonn
"Municipal Transportation Headquarters"

3 slides of W W I soldiers in the trenches

1 slide of a page from "Thomas Wright's Account
Book" (created for production, modified from
Henry Will Account Book, compiled by Donald L
Fennimore, Masthof Press (Route 1, Box 20,
Morgantown, PA 19543), © 1996)

1 slide of Joseph Wright's painting, _The Earthstopper_

4 slides "zooming in" on the image of "a man in
a funnel-shaped hat" (The image for the Off-
Broadway production came from _Jewish Art,
Grace Cohen Grossman, Hugh Lauter Levin
Associates, Inc,_ © 1995, _The Schocken Institute for
Jewish Research, Jerusalem,_ but other sources exist
for similar images)

1 slide of a Wandering Jew (_Zebrina Pendula_)
houseplant

1 slide of Beijing

1 slide of a smaller Chinese city (to stand in for
Dingtao)

1 slide of an old map of Poland with "Zabludow"
circled

1 slide depicting a gathering of anti-czarist
protesters (production image came from *Image
Before My Eyes, Lucjan Dobroszycki and Barbara
Kirshenblatt-Gimblett, Schocken Books,* © *1977,
p 110)*
1 slide depicting the "ethnographic surveyor"
(production image came from *Image Before My
Eyes (see above), p 17)*
1 slide of Sydney Australia
1 slide of rural Australia (for "outside Brisbane")
1 slide of the Acropolis in Athens
1 slide of a bathroom stall
1 slide of a rock on the coast of a Norwegian town
1 slide of a totem pole in Alaska
1 slide of a Mayan temple
1 slide of a park bench
1 slide of a statue on Easter Island
1 slide of a drawing of roman ruins with a
drawing of moths almost imperceptible in
the corner
3 slides "zooming in" on the moths, to see,
imprinted backward on the brown of the wing,
the white vestige of words (This was created
for production using clip art of roman ruins
combined with the image of a moth with words
imprinted on its wing, from author's private
collection)
1 slide depicting the Trylon and Perisphere from
the New York World's Fair of 1939
1 slide depicting the time capsule exhibit from that
fair